Full

this book is dedicated to all the people and places that helped me truly succeed along the way:

to my parents, Robin and Dathan, who blogged when I was little, loved me well, and inspired me to long to write;

to my brother, Aaron, whose artistic and musical talents make me want to be better;

to the community I've found at Covenant College over the past year and a half, who have kept me going through anxiety, depression, hard classes, and foggy days;

to the counselors I've had over the years, who have helped me shift my focus to the One who keeps me afloat in all the mess;

to those who believed in me, encouraged me to keep writing, and jumped around in excitement (or showed their excitement in a more socially acceptable way) when I told them I was writing my first book;

I love y'all.

Acknowledgements

I would like to thank those who taught me how to write well and suffered (thanklessly) through my comma errors, bad thesis statements, and run-on sentences: Renee Fuller and Susan Payne.

I would like to thank my professors at Covenant College who took my knowledge of writing and helped to turn it into something that I love so much more than coffee: Dr. Robert Erle Barham, Dr. Cliff Foreman, and Dr. Gwen Macallister.

I would like to thank all of the pastors, teachers, professors, and speakers I've listened to throughout my life because, without all of you, I would not have any background knowledge with which to bolster my writing.

I would like to thank my roommate, Natalie Abernathy for supporting this endeavor from the first day I told her about it during my freshman year of college— without that support, I never would have continued to write, and this book would never have come to completion.

Full

Abigail Sorrow

Table of Contents

Preface

This book is something I've dreamed about for a long time. When I was in kindergarten, I was moved up to a reading group with first grade kids, and my teacher apparently noticed that I loved to write. She challenged me to write a book, and thus came my first written work: *The Three Dogs*.

Since then, I have started and stopped writing things (these later projects were definitely of greater stock than my first "novel"), and I haven't really been able to bring anything to fruition until now.

As a college student, it's difficult to find time to write for fun. But today (October 23, 2018), I finally finished the almost-final proofing of the book, and I threw the paper copy up that had been heavily doctored in the air in excitement. It's been a long time coming.

As I've found recently, I suffer a lot with anxiety and depression. I had my first anxiety attack when I was a freshman in college: it was November 2, 2017. I talk about that a lot in the book, though, so stay tuned.

In the midst of the fall semester of my sophomore year in college, however, I started to struggle with depression. It seemed like I was stuck in this fog that I couldn't escape. Sometimes it lasts for hours, sometimes it lasts for an entire day. The first time I thought about committing suicide, I didn't know what to do, and when I feel like that now, I still don't know what to do in the moment. I've figured out how to care for my anxiety because that's something like old news. It seems to happen pretty often now. Stress sends me over the edge, so I do things that relieve stress for me: writing, cleaning, listing, organizing, being productive.

But this depression has been something new. I've realized over the past month or so, though, that writing is something that's more therapeutic than I thought. I did most of my work this semester on *Full* when I was trying to get out of the hole depression thrust me into.

Though my depression doesn't have a specific place in this book (it may in an upcoming book), some of the same concepts apply. Depression can be helped significantly by trusting in Christ— at least that's what I've discovered this past semester— and, as you'll read, that's something with which I struggle.

Writing this book has been as good for me as I hope reading it will be for you. My goal is not to sell a ton of copies (though that would be nice) or reach a ton of people with my first book (again, that would still be nice). My goal with *Full* is to reach YOU: the person who is holding this bound thing in their hand right now.

In the chapter called "Smart" I talk about legitimate success. In producing this book, I've even further realized my shortcomings in that area. Part of me wants to sell a lot of copies and baffle all the people who said that I wouldn't sell any copies of my first book (because no one knows who I am apart from my friends and family, which makes total sense), and the other part of me wants to be humble, reach who the Lord wants me to reach, and be fine with that.

In beginning this journey through my life, I would ask that you pray for my heart. Pray that I won't be consumed with the number of people that I reach, but that I will be consumed with the quality of the Lord's work in my life. I hope you find this journey somewhat parallel to your own, and if not, then I hope you find it complementary in just the right way.

So, as you begin reading, here's to finding fullness in Christ. Here's to recognizing that looking for fullness in the wrong places will only serve to provide momentary happiness. What you want is the true joy that comes with seeking Christ first and foremost, and I hope this memoir helps you to figure out how to do that.

Introduction

To doubt that the Lord is at work is to doubt the very nature of God. In His goodness, He provides all that we need, and He rescues us. Even the stars sing His praise each night as they gleam, impressing the darkness of the night sky with tiny, beautiful fragments of white light.

I also believe the Lord has called me as well as all Christians to something more than just remaining lukewarm in the faith. Why remain where I am in my Christian walk, though it may be a decent place, when I can be renewed by further realizing God's work in my life? Why should I downplay the things God has been teaching me by simply brushing them under the rug, leaving them to be fond memories of me just getting better? Why should I live as if God does not deserve all the glory I'm capable of giving him?

It's these questions that led me to write this book. The Lord gave me a heart for writing, so I started a blog a couple of years ago, but the topic of this book— seeking fullness in Christ alone— has been brought to the forefront of my mind so often in the past year that I decided I should go more in depth with it and share my story.

This book has foundations in the book of Ecclesiastes, and I also happen to love the book of Ecclesiastes. I remember reading it when I was a senior in high school, and I soaked in all the words, feeling like I couldn't get enough. It may have been because it was finally something I understood on my own apart from what my Christian school was teaching me, and it may have just been because it's a beautiful piece of literature. Either way, the Lord led me to it, so I read it, annotated it, and let it sit for a little while. Then I went on a retreat as a counselor for middle school girls, and, lo and behold, the topic was Ecclesiastes. The Lord kept revealing, and I kept absorbing, growing, and flourishing.

Yet there are days when I don't flourish. There are days when I feel like I'm slipping back into my past—back into the place from which the Lord pulled me and rescued me. There are times when I feel further away from God than I've ever felt. There are days when I feel like I can't trust Him, and there are days when I feel like He doesn't have my best interest in mind. I've even felt these things when doing something like being a camp counselor at a Christian day camp. One of my emptiest times spiritually was over the summer that I worked for such a day camp, and that was because I wasn't actively pursuing growth in my walk with Christ.

Over my first Christmas break of my time in college, I could not wait to go back to school. I wanted to be immersed in my friends, my classes, and the general joy present there on Lookout Mountain. However, the reunions I had with my friends were not as dramatic as I thought. As soon as I returned, the relationships

I thought were budding into actual friendships all seemed to fall apart. On the fourth day of classes, I realized that almost everyone around me was getting into relationships. Most of my close friends were either dating someone or were on the verge of dating someone, a lot of people from home were engaged and getting married, and it seemed like every time I would go anywhere on campus everyone would be holding hands with each other and just in general being close to another human of the opposite gender.

And then there was me.

In the typical style of teenage girls, I felt extremely alone and left out. I felt like not a single person was interested in me, and I would definitely graduate college alone. You know, I was mad at God. I was mad at the situation He had me in, and it just made me more angry to think about the fact that He is completely right all the time. I knew that He had my best interest in mind, but I didn't believe it in the slightest. My mom graciously told me that God had a plan, and I just didn't believe her. I remember sitting in my car after driving back from the gym and calling my mom, utterly perplexed about the purpose of my situation. She told me there was a guy out there for me, and she gave me a lot of examples of people who were still single or who were not dating around in college. I hung up the phone in anger, and as soon as I arrived at the dining hall, I saw one of my best friends having dinner with someone alone, and later on that night I found out that one of my best friends from home got engaged. Neither of those things were necessarily bad, but in my heart, I couldn't understand them. There was no one even close to being interested in me, and I felt the weight of that burden more heavily as I ate with my roommate and she tried to figure out what was wrong.

I tried to tell her, but I didn't express how genuinely distressed I was. I didn't express how much I wanted to curl up in a corner and cry. I felt extremely inferior—like I was worrying about something stupid. Like I had no right to feel sorry for myself. Holding in all the emotions I was feeling was not helping those emotions, so that's why I decided to start writing about it. I definitely did not trust God in those moments. I didn't want to believe that I had to wait. I knew it in my head, but I couldn't convince my heart.

But knowing it doesn't make any difference at all. I was still in the same situation, and I was significantly less content, and I had the additional problem of not believing in the all-sovereign power of God to work every single thing out for the good of those whom He loves.

God, however, has a way of being more faithful than we could ever imagine. He brought me into His perfect rest for a time then sent me back out into the world to tackle my problems. C. S. Lewis says this so beautifully in his book *Mere Christianity*:

> "The first step is to recognize the fact that your moods change. The next is to make sure that, if you have once accepted Christianity, then some of its main doctrines shall be deliberately held before your mind for some time every day. That is why daily prayers and religious readings and church-going are necessary parts of the Christian life. We have to be continually reminded of what we believe. Neither this belief nor any other will automatically remain alive in the mind. It must be fed. And as a matter of fact, if you examined a hundred people

who had lost their faith in Christianity, I wonder how many of them would turn out to have been reasoned out of it by honest argument? Do not most people simply drift away?"[1]

The training wheels were slowly coming off, but I felt like I still needed them on most occasions.

This book is my journey from the stage of training wheels into my life now. It's dirty and rugged around the edges. It's not clean-cut. But the story is beautiful in an imperfect way, and that's all because of my Jesus.

In his book, *A Grief Observed*, C. S. Lewis says this:

"He sees because he loves, and therefore loves although he sees."[2]

That totally resonates with me now that I return to it because it is such a testament to our desperate need for a Savior to make our ugly stories beautiful, even though we absolutely do not deserve it. I'll give it to you straight: as I said, my story is a mess. It's full of me going back and forth between satisfaction and dissatisfaction, between right and wrong, and between absolute joy and absolute sadness. But I know that Jesus is bigger than that.

I don't understand why I'm extremely wishy-washy. I don't get my emotions sometimes. I don't understand why I suffer. But God is bigger and better than all that, and this book is a combination of me trying to learn to be satisfied in my current situation and me trying to teach you what the Lord is teaching me. We never stop learning things about God because that would be impossible.

Pretty

Before I was old enough to care much about beauty, my dad told me I was beautiful, my mom did the same, as well as the rest of my family. I was built on a foundation of solid affirmation, yet I still did not believe it. I began to give in to the lies coming in hard all around me when I was about ten or eleven, and I simply decided to stop believing what my family would tell me.

Around fourth or fifth grade, I was a sight. I won't lie to you, I'm sure it was hard for my parents to tell me I was beautiful with my thick-rimmed glasses, the huge gap between my two front teeth, and my atrocious hair cut. That's when it started. I was never a part of the popular group of girls in my class, and I was never friends with the boys in my class. It began to sink in: I wasn't pretty, I wasn't good enough, I would never measure up.

I was in fifth grade, and this same cycle continued into sixth grade, seventh grade, eighth grade.

Middle school was the worst time for

me: the lowest I had ever been. My confidence was slashed by the fact that I had very few friends, and I began to hold a very low opinion of myself in general. I would look in the mirror and see feet too big, legs too long and skinny, ribs too prominent, wrists too small, acne-stricken skin, yellow teeth almost covered with the braces I'd had for what seemed like forever, hair too frizzy.

I would sit in class, on the verge of being in high school, still feeling friendless, and feel sorry for myself. My teacher even noticed and talked to my mom about it. I was left cherishing the short spurts of time when I would feel included and feeling utterly defeated when those times would end and I would find myself right back where I was before.

I once wrote in my journal after I had an encounter with a boy who did not feel the same as me that "I felt super valued... and now it's gone." I let his opinion and so many others' opinions define me. I asked so many times why no one was interested in me. I had tried to fix myself for them, forcing myself to be more outgoing. However, then I would assume I was annoying, so I would retreat back into my shell and remain silent. Then I asked myself if I was just ugly, weird, or something undesirable. I assumed the only solution to my problem was to change my outer appearance and my personality, and when that did not work, I decided that I was just unlovable, and that was it.

Then one day, some of that just went away almost as quickly as it had set in. I was on a retreat with my church in Colorado, and I began to feel worthy. I felt beautiful. Practically, it took a haircut. Spiritually, it took a little time spent with the Lord, but I made it there. I had no idea where it came from. I wrote this in my journal:

"I don't know, but I felt God in me that day. I literally went home and felt like a girl I always wanted to be."

I finally saw myself as beautiful. I was worth something.

I think all this stemmed from falling at the feet of Jesus, crying out in desperation. I remember sitting on a rock and doing a quiet time in our camp books, and the book prompted me to say a prayer. Honestly I think I was being dramatic. Because I felt so left out and so undesirable, I thought that having a story to tell or having something big happen to me would fill up the hole. I thought that having some huge spiritual encounter would cause me to be loved by someone. The thing is, I didn't care about what God had in store for me. I didn't care that I was supposed to let God create my story. I just cared that I had a story.

But God. As it says in Ephesians, "But God." Even though my motives were messed up and even though I came to Jesus and prayed from a position of pride, God still provided. He still gave me the story I wanted and needed. He was still so good to me. Even though my prayer came from a place of selfish want, he answered it in the most beautiful way possible, and he answered it quickly.

I don't think I fully grasped the concept of fullness in Christ at that point. I always had the question in the back of my mind of how one gets fulfilled. It echoed as I walked through the halls at school, and it reverberated through my mind as I sat quietly, but I could never place its meaning. I had no idea it would play such an important role in my testimony in the future.

I began to grow in my faith as a result of my newfound confidence, and I increased the time I spent with God. It wasn't perfect, and it still is absolutely not perfect, but I'm trying my best— which is all God asks of us because He knows that's all we're capable of. I began to think more about God and ponder my faith, which is key in forming a relationship with Him. Though I didn't intentionally start doing a quiet time until I was more than halfway done with high school, my faith grew in small ways until that point, then it took a drastically beautiful and faithful leap into a more mature Christian walk.

That's all that we imperfect children of God can do.

As I entered into the later years of my time in high school, I became even more confident in my worth in Christ, though I did still have days when I felt so bad about myself that I just wanted to curl up under a blanket and cry. As I began to read Ecclesiastes, almost all the doors were opened for me. I saw in that book that everything fades. Ecclesiastes 3:19-20 says this:

"For what happens to the children of man and what happens to the beasts is the same; as one dies, so dies the other. They all have the same breath and man has no advantage over the beasts, for all is vanity. All go to one place. All are from the dust, and to dust all return."

I knew that looks faded with age. I had always heard that you should be attracted to someone's heart first, but even their kindness fades. Kindness from a human standpoint is imperfect. Meaningless. Like wind. It sounds depressing, but people will always let us down, and we will always let others down, no matter how hard we try. That's just the unfortunate, totally depraved nature of mankind.

If we are seeking our fulfillment in the way we look or act, then we are seeking it in the wrong place. We are sorely mistaken, and we will be let down. Just as the middle school version of me, shrouded by my lack of confidence, sought fullness in what I looked like and was completely let down each time I glanced in the mirror or looked back at a photograph of myself, so you'll indefinitely be let down if you focus your entire life on something so fleeting as your appearance.

This principle extends also to reputation. I've spent a large portion of my life trying to please people because I have a fear of letting people down. I placed a lot of my worth in what people think, and that only weighs me down. Carrying around a suitcase of facades, pretty words, and nice thoughts only serves to slow my steps until I come to a screeching halt in front of the fact that I can't do it any more. I glance at my feet, sore from carrying the weight of appearances, and I shift my gaze to all the ground I've covered. But I've traveled in a circle, and I'm back to where I started.

I was stuck holding on to something that has nothing to hold onto, itself. Relying on reputation, looks, or any material thing to fill my spirit with joy will always come as an unfruitful search, a failing journey to a lost destination.

However, there is hope in the midst of the inevitable failure in a search for fulfillment in these places. That hope can be found in the fact that we, as imperfect humans, are not tasked with fulfilling ourselves. That's impossible. We cannot and should not ever seek joy and life in our looks and what people think about us because, again, those are two of the many, many things that simply do not have any internal support.

There was a new hotel under construction in my hometown. Since it's right next to the sidewalk facing the river, my friends and I passed it often. When I think about a hotel being built, in my mind the rooms are just plain squares with nothing in them but sawdust. I picture the hotel being supported from the inside with the walls between each room, but I don't see anything else.

When I walked past this new hotel, I saw something very different: posts. There were countless posts lined up inside the cinder-block structure supporting each floor, keeping the entire building from caving in on itself. It was not incredibly pretty, but I knew it was safe.

Things that will fulfill you are steady, supported internally. The only thing that is perfectly supported and completely safe housing for our trust is God, so God is the only thing in which we should place our trust and find satisfaction for which we long. No, it isn't pretty to have an obstructed view to the other side of that hotel. It's not pretty when something is being built up because it's unfinished, but when it's finished it's glorious. Not only is it secure and practical (most of the time), but it's also beautiful and functional (again, most of the time). That's how we are going to be when we cross into Heaven, except there won't be a chance that we won't be perfect, and there definitely won't be a chance that we won't be complete and secure. It's not pretty on earth to be torn apart every day by the world, to be tested constantly, to be insecure and afraid. It does not feel pretty to seek joy in a God who sometimes seems to be ignoring us, but is safe and fool-proof, and we can be sure of our renewal and remaking in our heavenly home where we'll dwell for eternity. Our orders are just this:

perfect demands from a perfect demander. The scars are being made beautiful in the demands of the world, and we can always be assured that the scars will be removed once we reach eternity.

Seek fullness in who you are under the most perfect influence. Seek fullness in who Christ is. That's the only definite way to be joyful, and trying to find satisfaction and contentment anywhere else will bring less than desirable results.

One final thing I'll say about this is that being attractive and having a good reputation are not bad things, and they aren't things that we should necessarily forsake. These things, along with many of the other things I'll talk about in this book are good things when seen or used in moderation. When they aren't balanced with humility and an outstanding, overarching love for Christ, they become sinful, losing that goodness with which they should be associated. Being beautiful and well-liked is not sinful because those are things with which the Lord has blessed us. But when we allow those things to define how much we love Christ, then we fall into what is being discussed in this chapter. That's when beauty become bad.

It is not a sin to be an attractive or well-liked person. In fact, we are seen as beautiful by the Lord, and we are loved by God. But that's the kicker. When we allow the love of others to outshine the love of Christ in our hearts, then we are headed down the wrong path. Find your identity in the way the Lord sees you rather than the way the world sees you, and you're finding fulfillment in Christ. When you seek satisfaction in how the world sees you, then you're stuck basing your life on something that will, without a doubt, fade away. In the end, your looks fade, your personality fades, your family's personalities fade, your friends' personalities fade. But God does not fade. When you base your life on something that will fade away, then you're doomed to fade away as well. When you base your life on the One who gives you life, then you're destined for His perfect success and perfect satisfaction that stems straight from the Vine.

Smart

When you stick a label on a drawer or a file or something like that, it's pretty hard to remove because labels are made to stick. You can pull it off sometimes, depending on the material, but there's always residue, even if there's just a very vague shape left behind. The same goes for people: when you label them with something that seems to fit their personality, then they tend to end up being stuck with that label for a long time. Even when people remove that label or you remove yourself from those who are labeling you, there's still some residue left over from what was one stuck to you. Back in elementary school, I would make perfect scores on every math test, I would always get picked to be in the spelling bee, and I would usually win the bee fairly easily— a relative term— after hours and hours of spelling the same words over and over with my mom.

"Precipice," she'd probe.

"Precipice, P-R-E-C-I-P-I-C-E, precipice."

My responses were mechanical at best. Say the word, spell the word, say the word. And "be perfect" was the hidden fourth step in the process.

I was quickly labelled the "smartest kid in the class," and I allowed that label to define me. But instead of labelling me, it became me. In sixth grade, I moved up to a math class with some people I didn't even know in the eighth grade. Eventually, I made friends with the people in the class, and everything was fine, but I still felt like I had to fully accomplish what my labels made me. I had to remain the smartest person in the class, or else I would let people down, I would be ashamed, I would never recover. I remember being so embarrassed to receive low grades back then that I wouldn't show anyone. I would just try to forget.

I constantly lived under pressure to live up to the standards, albeit impossible, that my peers set for me. I had to study hard so that I could keep my grades up— so that I could be as perfect as possible for the eyes staring me down all around me, seeming to be waiting for me to fail. Eventually, anxiety formed within me and spread around my body so that I writhed in it day in and day out. I had always had a guilty conscience, and I'm sure my parents thought it was weird when I would call them in my room at night to confess something I did months earlier that probably wasn't even a bad thing. I couldn't rest without knowing that I was living in what I thought was perfection. I developed a fear of failure. Each returned assignment would be met with my stomach doing flips inside of me anxiously awaiting the knowledge of whether I had the highest grade in the class or not. If I didn't, then I would actually feel guilty. I felt like I had let people down. I felt embarrassed because someone would ask me about my score, and when I would tell them they would express to me the fact that they were overjoyed because they had done the impossible in scoring higher than me. I also felt embarrassed when I did well because, again, people would curiously ask me what I scored, and I would hesitate to tell them, so they would guess. Aiming high in their guesses, they would assume perfection, and they would usually get it.

"Why are you so smart?"
"Abi, I don't even wanna hear it."
"Abi, I don't care."
"Abi, I hate you."

Well, you asked, I would think. I became an academic recluse, afraid to receive returned assignments for fear of people asking me what I scored. However, a very minuscule part of me felt happy when I would make high A's. I felt a secret little rush of satisfaction when a returned assignment would have a red "100" written across the top of the page.

I feared the day when my assignments would be less than perfect. I feared the day when I wouldn't be an integral part of a group project. When my math teacher started calling me out for making mistakes in AP Calculus, which I was taking as a junior in high school, I felt so destroyed. I tried to rationalize the whole situation to make myself feel better, telling myself that I would really buckle down and study harder next time, I would go to her and ask her for help, I would stop volunteering to do problems on the board so that I would stop being embarrassed when I made a mistake.

That day arrived as I began what I knew would be the most academically difficult year of my life. Junior year ushered in anxiety about the heavy class load I was about to take on, the upcoming college search, and my social situation. I attended the same school for fourteen years when I graduated, so most of my friends had been my friends for upwards of five or six years. Still, I didn't feel as if I had any true friends. I felt like I was just living in an environment with other people, and I didn't really have my own place. I was just a floater. I could have turned to my church, but the situation was the same there: people praised me for my golden character, yet rather than searching for my core group of friends at events, I was searching for whichever group was less intimidating and less uncomfortable.

Needless to say, I began the year with an extremely negative attitude. I was hateful toward my school as well as toward people who I did not enjoy being around. If it didn't go my way, then it was wrong. As an addition to the already negative mindset I had adopted, my plate was full, and I was tired and overworked.

I should have seen this coming. I should have seen the late nights turning into early mornings before all my work was done taking away from my time with the Lord. I should have seen myself being consumed, but I had to do the most and be the best, or else I would be a failure. I just knew it.

I reached my breaking point in November of 2015: the fall of my junior year. I had been through a lot during the first semester, and I had received low grade after low grade. One day, I received a grade, a C (with which I was very unfamiliar), and I was unsurprised because I knew I had done badly on the assignment. However, my best friend texted me to ask about my grade, and it turned out that he had done better than me. Moments later, I received another grade in that same class, and it, too, was less than what I expected. I broke down into tears. I laid my head down on my desk and sobbed a desperate, pitiful cry. I wasn't me. I was turning into someone I had never been before. My identity was crushed into a thousand tiny, tear-soaked pieces, and I didn't know how to sweep up those pieces and put them back together into a new creation. I couldn't recreate myself—only God could do that.

Finally, it clicked with me: my identity is not a grade. It sounds like a very elementary concept, and I was sure I had told someone to seek their identity in Christ before, but I never took my own words to heart. I resolved before my second semester to have a positive attitude about all aspects of my life. I was going to be intentional in seeking my identity in Christ, and I was going to be intentional in looking for a good thing in each day— especially the rough ones.

I became a new person: recreated by the One who created me in the first place. I stopped caring so much about grades. It still bothered me when people would respond rudely to my success, and it still bothered me when people would unintentionally tear me down because they hadn't done as well on an assignment as me, but I was slowly, surely getting over it. I was moving on from what had defined me for so many years, and I was free. I finally found a place where I could thrive, so I took it, and I ran with it. I sprinted away from grades into the arms of the Father—the only thing, I finally realized, that could fill me up and define me.

At this point in my life, I wrote my testimony down seriously for the first time. The verses I randomly came across in my Bible were from Psalm 22. David is crying out to God here, and to me it sounded eerily familiar. It sounded like the voice of my shallow sobs on my desk that night. It sounded like the voice of my embarrassment at receiving a low grade, and the frustration that cyclically followed. It sounded like the voice of my hostility toward my family out of sheer exhaustion. It sounded like the depths of my soul crying out for help while my body denied my need for it.

> "My God, my God, why have you forsaken me? Why are you so far from saving me, from the words of my groaning? O my God, I cry by day, but you do not answer, and by night, but I find no rest. Yet you are holy, enthroned on the praises of Israel. In you our fathers trusted; they trusted, and you delivered them. To you they cried and were rescued; in you they trusted and were not put to shame." (vv. 1-5)

I realized that my identity had been found in what others thought and in how successful I was in my endeavors, and then I resolved to stop defining success in accordance with the world. I resolved to stop seeing myself as a number, a student, a child of my own work. I saw myself as a child of God, first and foremost, doing what He called me to do in the best way I knew how. I was on an upward path. I was steadily learning how to seek my identity and fullness in Christ rather than in the world, and that helped me to see hard things as good things. I was learning how to be satisfied in my position. I was learning to rejoice in academic success because it was a blessing from God, and I was learning to stop despairing in academic failure because that's not what made me Abigail.

Academic success is something that is from the Lord, and it pleases Him when we use our talents to glorify Him. It sounds contradictory to say that you should try to do well in school and work. Try to be successful, but don't let it kill you. Don't let it reduce you to tears. Don't let it take away the joy behind the gift of academia. It isn't glorifying to God to take what He has given us and replace Him. We are called to find our identity in Him, but when we seek it out in something He has given us as a tool with which we can glorify Him further, we are not pleasing Him. Though the Lord does not need our praise, He demands it, and to take that away from Him is a sin, plain and simple.

Flash forward to the summer after my freshman year of college: I had committed to work at a traveling day camp all summer. I was excited about it when I got hired back in October, but then as the summer got closer and closer I began to get nervous. What would I do if I changed too much over the summer and people at home thought I was weird when I got back? What if I lost all my friends when I got back to school because of the limited communication? Would I even be able to succeed if I was changing locations all summer and having to learn kids' names on the same day that I had met them?

All these questions met me as I arrived at training. I wanted to succeed, and I felt like the job I was given was something at which I could succeed, but my problem was fear. All the fears I listed earlier and more were standing in my shadow, waiting to jump on me when I finally thought I was having fun and making friends. I was afraid that my team would think I was weird or that we wouldn't click (and the fact that we would be spending a little more than eleven weeks working closely together does not make that a fun thought). I was afraid that the Holy Spirit would tell me something I did not want to hear. I was afraid that my relationship with my boyfriend would be hurt instead of helped by the distance. I was afraid that I wasn't as good at leading kids as I thought I was. I was afraid, plain and simple.

But God.

As the week of training went on, I felt like everything was going to be ok. I felt amazing about my team, and I felt like God and I were on pretty much the same page. I woke up each morning excited to learn more things about my job and about my coworkers. It seemed like I had been placed on the team that best fit my personality, and I was excited to get to know all of the people I was about to spend ten weeks working with. I still woke up a little earlier in the morning to read my Bible. I looked forward to the day when camp became just *camp* rather than my summer job. I heard from so many speakers on our theme for the summer, which directly applied to my life in so many ways, which meant that I should (theoretically) be successful in teaching children about it. When we left for our first location, I was happy to receive my phone and laptop back, but I wasn't suffering without it. I missed my boyfriend and my family, but it seemed like I could live without direct communication with them for a little while.

For a time, it seemed like this summer was going to be a breeze.

Then the first week of camp happened. We drove from Rome, Georgia, to Daytona Beach, Florida, arriving a day earlier than we usually arrive at a location for a week of camp in order to figure out how to set things up and meet our hosts. I loved the hosts immediately, and things seemed to be going well. I was told that I was team-teaching my skill (which meant that, even though my cooking skill usually had two skill rooms because of the large volume of kids who wanted to do it, the other teacher and I would be combined in one room and just given all the kids who wanted to do it all at once), and I was happy. I was ready, as my anxieties seemed to fade away into a distant memory from a time before I knew what to expect.

When Sunday rolled around, however, I found myself stressed out. I remember arriving back at our hotel late Sunday night, after a long day of two church services and setting up camp for the first time, with instructions to be on the vans at 5:00 AM. I walked back to my room, eyes filled with impending tears, and I tried to get to bed as quickly as possible. I didn't know how I was going to do it, I told my boyfriend, my voice shaking because I was trying to hold back my tears. He'd never seen me cry.

By the end of the week, I had led some cheers, painted my entire face green, danced on stage to every song (because I'm a motions leader), led ten small groups, and taught twelve skills, had shaving cream piled on my head before flossing on stage in front of a bunch of kids and adults, cheered about my small group animal while walking across parking lots, and gotten a pretty impressive watch tan. But I felt like something was missing. I wasn't feeling very encouraged. I felt like I was doing a good job, but even when I was in tears on the recreation field outside because I had lost my voice from all the cheering and my kids weren't listening, I felt very alone. It's hard to feel alone when you live with twenty-seven other people in a hotel for a week and have amazing host churches who attend to your every need, but I felt it more than I'd ever felt it before.

I felt like I wasn't succeeding because no one was telling me I was succeeding. And, sure, I may not have been doing amazing because it was my first week of camp, and I was basically clueless, but I felt like I was at least doing something right, and I wasn't getting recognized for it.

It was a new feeling. Before I went to college, encouragements rained down on me, and that was what I lived for. Like I said, I wanted to be right—I wanted to be perfect—and because I wasn't being encouraged on a momentary basis (which is a lot to ask), I felt like I was failing.

It wasn't until the fourth week, in Auburn, Alabama, (the one that inspired me to write the end of this section of the book) that I realized that I wasn't working at at this camp just so I could get affirmed and know that I was doing a great job. I decided to work there because God wanted to stretch me as far as I could go. He wanted to show me that there is so much more to life than being encouraged all the time (I'm not at all saying that I wasn't being encouraged—I was being poured into by my teammates constantly, I was just having trouble seeing it). He wanted to show me that I need to be working to please Him, not others. Working to please others for the first couple of weeks only led to more exhaustion than I was already experiencing.

The third week of camp was a full camp in Viera, Florida, which meant that I had twenty-four kids in my small group, and I was team-teaching forty kids for three skills per day, but that was the week that I really started having fun with the kids. It became less of a job and more like camp (with a few added responsibilities). I started cheering because I had to, and then I ended up loving it. I started telling stories in Cooking about where I got the ingredients, and I started loving it. I began to love dancing on stage with the rest of the motions team. I began to love my job.

I won't lie: there were a few nights where I wanted nothing more than to just go home, take a hot shower, climb into bed, and sleep for twenty-four hours straight. But at the end of the week, I realized that I love camp.

That was the success I was looking for. The next week, I feel like I really did succeed because I decided to have fun. I took pride in winning cheer-offs. I loved it when my campers in cooking believed my stories about my stuffed moose and the secret mission we had to take to get our cold ingredients— a cover-up for the fact that the refrigerator was all the way across the campus. I loved almost all of it, and that's how I succeeded.

You're not succeeding at all unless you are finding that success in how much you're glorifying God in the process of getting the task done. Throughout the summer I felt like a failure. There were days when I thought I was succeeding, but at the end of the day, someone else was praised, and I was quickly reminded of the mistakes I had made— each one coming before my mind's eye like a home movie, a memory that I can't seem to erase. But, looking back, it's not hard to see where I actually succeeded this summer. Through the post-camp months, the process of learning about the changes camp brought me has been a process of coming to terms with the hard successes I had: learning to cope with too much extroversion, learning to survive on less sleep just so I could read my Bible, gaining confidence by failing. Sometimes success comes from failure.

Love

I've always dreamt of a fairytale relationship for as long as I can remember, and I spent years of my life being dissatisfied with my singleness. I would pursue every opportunity, no matter how small, and usually I would end up hurt as a result of my overthinking things from the get-go. I just couldn't get past the point of thinking I wasn't good enough for anyone, and that's why I wasn't in a relationship. I saw a lot of my peers seeming to jump over the threshold of being "just friends" to being in a relationship with someone, and I couldn't understand why I was still in the "just friends" stage with so many people. I finally came to the conclusion that I wasn't cut out for a relationship because I didn't deserve it and no one could ever love me. It was a drastic realization, but I just assumed the worst.

However, during the fall of my senior year, I adopted a new state of mind. The previous summer was a summer of growth in which I learned more about how to be satisfied in Christ, though imperfectly. I became fine with being alone, when in the past I had spent most of my waking hours feeling lonely and sorry for myself. I was fine with my singleness, knowing that the Lord had someone for me, and I was fine with waiting. I wrote this on my blog:

"When the Lord calls you to wait, He's calling you to see His greater purpose. He's calling you to look for fulfillment in Him rather than that standard, or whatever your struggle may be. He's calling you to seek Him rather than that thing you've been praying for for the longest time. He's calling you to see that it's not really worth it to chase after trivial things when you could be chasing after Him."

I've often referred to this girl as the best version of me. She was the best version of me because I had finally made my way out of the swamp of heavy dissatisfaction, the mire of my lack of self-worth. She wasn't weighed down by not being good enough because she had adopted this new confidence that she'd never experienced before. She realized that God was working, and she was ready for Him to work on her until she was transformed into who He wanted her to be. To be this girl was amazing.

October thirteenth rolled around, and I was thriving. That morning, I confidently walked into our local coffee shop, clad in heels and a business-casual dress, ready to write a blog post and head to a conference I was attending later that morning. The only thing I really remembered from attending it the year before was the fact that its attendees are forced to socialize since seats are assigned, which would usually be very scary for me, but I had overcome that fear— at least for a moment— and I was determined to make friends.

But it was an unusually confident day. Upon arriving at the conference, I cautiously made my way to my seat, and I sat down and started socializing. I was proud of myself. Wasn't this just the biggest blessing? The Lord was finally giving me the confidence to talk to a stranger, and I felt more confident than I'd ever felt. I was almost giddy. I started talking to the person sitting next to me, and we really hit it off.

That night, he messaged me, and a day did not go by in which we did not speak for a little over two months. Those two months were full of me falling head over heels for this guy , but I was falling out of love with something else.

Too fast. It was all moving too fast. I said to all my questioning friends and family that he was just being intentional, which I appreciated. He was just pursuing me with a purpose, and, even though we weren't yet dating, I figured that the relationship was headed in a good direction. The day arrived, and I went on my first date with essentially a stranger in whom I placed a good bit of trust. At the end of our first date, I began to fall, and from that moment on I was tumbling. I was quick to tell all my friends about "how sweet" the date was, and I was so happy. I was over the moon. I was ecstatic. It was finally my turn to be truly happy, I thought. I told myself that this was the goal I had been reaching for, and I had finally achieved it.

I felt like a queen almost every time we spoke, and when I saw him, which was about once a week because of the distance, I would return home with the biggest smile plastered across my face. True joy was what I thought I had attained. I thought the Lord was using the warp speed at which this relationship was traveling to show me that this guy was *the one*.

A week or two after our first date, I went to his house by myself for the first time. My parents were hesitant, which made me unusually angry, even though they had every right to hesitate. It was fine. It was normal to argue with parents about boyfriends and relationships. Right? I arrived at his door and then we left the house to explore his city. After a short drive around and a quick meal, we drove back to his house. From there, I moved onto the path toward the downward spiral that defined the majority of this relationship.

It wasn't a good idea. I saw my boundaries fade into the distance as I ran so far away from them. As long as I had some semblance of morality, though, I was ok, I thought. It was permissible, and I was enjoying my new life. I'd never been *this girl* before.

We drove up to the overlook at the mountain on the outskirts of his town, and we watched the sun setting over the tree-line. Romantic, yes. However, we continued to skirt on the line of my own boundaries, as I simply forgot them. I began to forget who I was, and I turned into the girl I feared the most.

I knew, in the back of my mind, that it was wrong. I knew that we needed to focus on the spiritual side. We decided from the beginning to center our relationship on Christ, but that is immensely difficult when the physical side of the relationship is so much more attractive in the moment.

After church, we were alone in his house. From there, I picked up again and sprinted away from my previously set boundaries. I assumed I was still up on my own little pedestal of morality. I assumed that I could focus equally on pursuing a relationship with God and a relationship with this guy. My relationship with Christ turned into one that consisted of checking off the box of my quiet time, praying a small prayer thanking God for this guy, and then falling asleep because I stayed up late the night before texting him. God was not only placed on the back burner, but He became the back burner. He became a mere pawn: someone I claimed to trust with everything until things started to fall apart, and then I blamed Him, asking Him why on earth He would be testing me, "His faithful child."

Our relationship coasted downhill until January. I was in the worst place I've ever experienced: moody, hostile, obsessed, insecure, angry, confused. Most of these negative emotions were aimed at God. I felt what seemed to be a physical pain in the pit of my stomach for the longest time, and it felt like the pain I feel when I get really anxious about something. It felt like someone was slowly constricting my insides and not allowing me to move. I thought I was afraid of commitment (I am, but that wasn't the root). I thought this could be solved with a simple conversation that would turn into something more than that. I thought this could be solved with affirming words, so I peppered him with all the reasons why I liked him, hoping to convince myself of those reasons along the way.

One night, the discomfort took away my sleep, so I prayed seriously for the first time in a long time. I grabbed some paper and wrote it down.

"Lord, I really need you. I always really need you, but now it's gotten to the point where I can't do anything. My relationship with you is crap, honestly. I haven't truly prayed in about a month, and I hate that. It's killing me. I think I have the illusion of being truly happy, but I'm not. I'm second-guessing everything I do. Every time I think too much about my relationship, I get doubtful...I believe you brought him into my life for a reason. I believe that you are sovereign over all, so PLEASE give me peace. My heart is literally hurting because of this. I don't want this to be over."

I didn't want to admit it. I was feeling the Holy Spirit telling me to leave this thing that was holding me back. The pain, the discomfort in my gut wasn't dismissible. Trust me, I tried to dismiss it. I dismissed it for almost two months because my relationship with God had become so solid. Thinking of living without this guy in my life made me want to cry because he had become my life. He had become a god to me. I told myself it wouldn't happen, but it happened as soon as I allowed myself to be a little freer and go a little further than I thought was right. Be a little less moral. I thought God was content being on my back burner because "at least I was still partially pursuing Him."

God doesn't want a partial pursuit.

After spending a couple of weeks ignoring the urging of the Spirit in my soul, I broke down. I lost my composure, and I just cried. I knew what I had to do, and I definitely did not want to do it. I wanted to stay in my comfortable position. We talked about my birthday, prom, and graduation, and I thought all that stuff would be hard and disappointing without him to celebrate with me. To be without this big part of my life was unthinkable, but I still called him late one night and told him that I didn't think things were going to work. I told him frankly that I did not know why in the world

I was feeling this way, and I cried from the moment he said hello to me on the phone. After a very long conversation, he said to let it sit overnight and see how I felt in the morning. I hung up, then I watched a video about listening to your conscience, and I was further convicted. I knew what I needed to do, but I decided to sleep on it and give the relationship one more chance to redeem itself.

The next day, I texted him to tell him it was over. I told him I wished it didn't have to be this way, and he said he knew, and that was the end. All of a sudden I stopped being fulfilled. The hole was empty again. As soon as I laid my phone down after that last conversation—if you could even call it a conversation— I felt a very large, festering wound reopen. I felt the skin being pulled back to reveal the messiness inside, and I knew it would take lots of repair if I was ever going to be normal again.

The Holy Spirit speaks to Christians. He works in so many ways. According to Wayne Grudem,

> "Scripture talks about a day-to-day guidance by the Holy Spirit—being 'led' by the Holy Spirit, and walking according to the Spirit."[3]

The things that Christians do and feel as they make decisions are a result of the Lord's work. Our impulses come from the Spirit, and while they may be difficult to follow, they should always be the priority.

I felt at peace about my decision, but I began to feel a different type of pain. As the psalmist in Psalm 77:4 says,

> "You hold my eyelids open; I am so troubled that I cannot speak."

The pain resulted from a hatred of who I had become, a hatred of the fact that I had just forsaken almost all my boundaries and become a doormat for just two months of temporary happiness, a hatred for what seemed like just a big waste of time. The pain was more of a "what have I done?" kind of pain, and that's the best way I can describe it. I longed for what had become my life for the past months. I longed to undo it all because that was just another failure I had under my belt. I didn't want to face my friends or my family out of embarrassment. I didn't even want to look at myself, eyes puffy from crying so much, ashamed of the girl I had become.

The most beautiful phrase in the Bible to me is "But God" in Ephesians 2:4. It presents the most beautiful contrast to who we are as a people: broken, incomplete, unworthy. It creates a picture of what is to come when we are physically reunited with the Father in Heaven, and I find that incredibly encouraging. Thinking about all the sinful acts I've committed, all the hearts I've broken, all the people I've let down, causes me to look within and see blackness and death. I see the fact that I could truly never measure up, as I've feared for my whole life. I see the fact that I am truly dead in my sin, and I deserve absolutely nothing good. However, I see the beauty of the *but* in Ephesians 2:4, and I have peace in my troubled spirit.

In this struggle, the Lord met me. I was unable to move any further on my own, trapped and held down by my own wants, so the Lord picked me up, supported me, and rescued me. Trampled like the psalmist in Psalm 56:1 by the shame I had when thinking back on the things I had done as well as the fear of what people would think if they found out, my spirit was broken. I carried a new, heavier burden of regret. The day that I ended things with this guy in whom I had completely invested the past two months, I cried. I remember sitting in my bathroom to hide my sobs from the rest of my family, sending the text, and just holding my head in my trembling palms, wondering what I had just done. Why did I just end the best thing that had ever happened to me?

Because it *wasn't* the best thing.

When you seek fullness in the wrong place for long enough, it becomes a lifestyle. It becomes your default just as it became my default. I couldn't imagine a day going by without a text to tell me good morning and affirm me in some way. I couldn't imagine a day going by without seeing his face.

He became my god, and I welcomed that sensation because it brought me a momentary pleasure, even though it was gone as soon as he was.

In reality, we should be unable to imagine a day going by without talking to God, without reading the Bible, without intentionally praising Him throughout the day. Unfortunately, that isn't the reality for a lot of us, including me. That isn't the reality because God doesn't seem as attractive as something we really want when it's placed in front of us.

But God.

God used this brokenness to open up a new pathway to spiritual health. The very same day, He brought into my life a community of friends and mentors so willing to help me get better. He made me want to have a quiet time each day. I would wake up each morning, and habitually check my phone for a new text from my now-ex-boyfriend only to be disappointed to the point of tears, so I would spend some extra time reading my Bible or listening to a sermon that I thought would help me. I can attest to the fact that the desire did not come from inside me at all. I, myself, wanted to run far away from God, back to this guy to whom I had given so much of myself, back to my bed where I could cry for days. But God gave me strength and filled me with his Spirit. He gave me the rare ability to thank Him sincerely for what happened. He allowed me to live mostly free from soul-crushing regret that I assumed would follow this relationship.

That's what ultimately led me to worship. I remember going to a retreat the weekend after it happened, and we sang the song "Good, Good Father," which took me back to all the times my worship leader had asked me to sing that song in church. It was the first song I ever led in front of the whole church, sweaty-nervous and voice trembling. Why? For such a time as this. Ecclesiastes 3:1 says,

"For everything there is a season, and a time for every matter under heaven."

I wrote on my blog after that weekend about how I realized that God really is good. I just needed to believe it. I needed to believe that He was a good Father because of all the things He puts in my path to test me, draw me closer to Him, make me love Him more than I ever could on my own.

Sometimes that "good," though, is not our own good. Sometimes the good things that God gives His children are things they may not want, things they may not think they need. Sometimes the good things God gives His children are things that seem painful at the time. It's like getting a limb amputated. You feel that the part of you that was once there is now gone, but then you realize that the part of you that it was necessary to remove only would've hurt you in the end. It's necessary pain, and that's the pain caused by God's immeasurable goodness to us. He wants us to be more like Him, so he removes parts of us that separate us from Him, even if that surgery is painful and seems to be unnecessary. He soothes us to sleep with the anesthesia of grace, promising that we'll wake up as good as new. He promises that we'll wake up closer to Him without the part of us that was once full of the infection of sin. Whether we wake up now, in a week, or in eighty years, we'll wake up at the right hand of God the Father, and it will be a glorious day.

With this event came a newly intense willingness to be vulnerable with people. I was not going to put up a facade of perfection. I was not going to act like this wasn't partially my fault. I knew I could use this story to help other people who were going through something similar, so the Lord placed me in a community with people who were having similar struggles. I realized the usefulness of the struggle in the difficulty of that struggle.

I tried to get back to the place I ruined for more than a year. A year after I met the boy who turned into my god, I found it. I found the place of satisfaction. I haven't discovered how to perfectly be fulfilled in what Christ is doing in my life—I don't believe anyone ever can—but I am imperfectly at a point in my life where I can confidently say that I love my life. I like where the Lord has me. And even though that place is consistently changing, I can always see some small hint at what the Lord wants for me there, and I can now more easily find the purpose of the location.

It's truly a monumental feeling. It feels like God scooped me up in His arms and said, "Abigail, that was good, but this is better." It's true that the time I spent getting close to God before I started that toxic relationship was good, and I do sometimes wish it had never ended. But the place I'm in now is so much better. He wanted the best for me, so He gave it to me— even though the journey was rough, and I spent a lot of that time in utter confusion.

I realized that losing my relationship with God, losing that fullness I can so easily find in the Savior, was not worth being so emotionally unsure, but it was not easy to come to this realization and put into action what I knew I needed to do. As I said, it's been a long time since the whole thing ended, and it took a long time to get back to a full place. I finally returned to a newly remodeled home, and as I set my bags in the corner next to the unfamiliar doorway, free from decorations and furniture, it still smelled like my old home. It still had some semblance of a familiar place. It was just better. It improved in the most perfect way possible, and it's a place I never want to leave, except when I get a heavenly upgrade.

However, if I know anything about God, I'm sure there are still renovations necessary to occur. I'm sure there's still something that needs to be done to fix who I am because I'm still myself. I haven't reached that heavenly place yet, so I'm still being transformed.

To end, I will say this: transformation hurts, but we can find beauty in the changing because that changing is coming straight from a God who never changes.

Time

I like to know what's going on, and that may be a problem. It's not a problem to appreciate schedules and organization, but it is a problem when you let that run your life, when you let the fact that not everything has a schedule ruin everything, when you worship your organized time, when you worship having it all together.

That's what I'm guilty of. I'm guilty of worshiping my time, and I'm guilty of finding fulfillment in having my life put together. Often, I find myself taking a lot of time to intentionally "get my life together," and I'm beginning to rethink the reason behind these sections of time. Why am I doing this? Is it out of necessity because I need to steward the resources God has given me? Or is it because I feel the need to be organized in order to feel good about myself and my status?

I find it very difficult to write about this topic. I think it's because it doesn't make any sense at all to worship something so fleeting. Time is literally passing by as I write and proofread, and I'll never see those seconds again. As they pass, I'm getting older. I'm literally watching the object of my worship pass away, yet I'm still worshipping it. I'm still placing my trust in how well I schedule my life even though it has such a negative effect on me. Because sometimes having too much on my plate helps me stay focused on getting things done, but sometimes it overwhelms me. Even though I may not have to do everything I have planned, it throws my day off when I can't complete my to-do list. It becomes a stressor.

It's like I'm worshipping garbage. I worked in facilities at my college, and I took out the trash once every day. It is still amazing (and slightly alarming) to me that such a small community of students who frequent the library could produce so much trash. By the time my second shift rolled around, the trash cans were no longer pristinely empty, and someone had already dropped a full cup of coffee without a lid into the trash can, forcing me to redo all the work I did earlier in the shift. Worshipping time and worshipping schedules is like worshipping a gum wrapper, an empty coffee cup, a used tissue: something that is used then tossed, only to be transferred into a dumpster and then taken to a landfill to rot. Time is fleeting, as is everything.

Satan has made me blind to that.

Seeking fullness in seeming to know what's going to happen and having your life together is simply destructive. It's only creating more and more stress that becomes so much harder to deal with after every bout. It's like alcohol. Schedules are addictive. Knowledge is addictive. When the addiction goes on for a long time, then it becomes harder to break.

I want to break that addiction. I want to finally be free from the bonds of time, the bonds of organization, the bonds of having my life together. The only way to do that is to give that time to Christ. Give your whole life to Christ. Without that aspect of your life, not only is all your scheduling and organizing meaningless—so is your entire life. Without Christ leading my steps, I would be headed nowhere.

Sometimes, though, I think I should be leading my own steps. Sometimes it seems like the Lord isn't looking out for me. When he was leading me out of a relationship, I felt like He was out to get me. I would never admit it, but I thought, deep down, that the Lord was leading me down a dark path that was meant to hurt me. He was messing with my own schedule for my life— as if it has ever been my own— so I was uncomfortable, and I felt very out of place. My time was slowly slipping out of my hands, and I was angry about it, honestly. I realized I was losing control, and I didn't like it. I realized I was not going to be able to make my own decisions, and I was scared. So all of that caused me to overcorrect and try to run my whole life myself. I thought I could do it without the Father leading my every step, and I was sorely mistaken.

As I spent days walking around my college campus still as a single girl, I couldn't help but wonder why God "hadn't come through for me yet." I questioned his judgment as I was continually not chosen to lead groups and activities. I became disheartened when I had yet another anxiety attack over something not worth worrying about. I doubted the goodness of what the Lord had in store for me. Sometimes it drives me crazy that I cannot get it through my head that God is in control. I know, in my head, that He's good, He's sovereign, and He's in control of every single thing that happens, and He's working it all out for my good and His glory. Somehow I can't believe it, though. There's this gap between what I know is true and what I believe is true, and I fall deep down into the gap when I let the fact that I don't have control over things get to me. When I dwell on the fact that I'm not going to be able to do exactly what I want when I want to, my feet slip and slide down the steep hill that leads into the darkest pit, and I can't seem to wrestle myself out of the stronghold of the pit.

My schedule is something that comes from my mind, and if it doesn't go along with God's, then that's out of my hands. In reality, it's always out of our hands because obviously I can't sit down and plan out every single little detail of my life, and neither can you. Our lives are always affected by the lives of others, which is a logical reason why. But in addition to that, God has planned every single detail of every single life that has ever existed. The Lord will have me do what He wants me to do, even if it isn't on my to-do list for the day. While that seems harsh of Him in our own eyes— shrouded by sin— we must remember that we are His. He is the creator of time, and the fact that we have the freedom to fill it is a gift not to be taken for granted. We didn't have to even be created. We don't have to exist, but we do, and that is by His grace alone.

Time is slipping away, and we act as if we can get a hold on it and manipulate it to fit our own bill. In reality, the only thing we should be reaching for is God, and even then we should not try to manipulate Him to fit our schedule— we should be content where we are and with the fact that God has our best interest in mind. We need only to wait for Him and His absolutely perfect timing. Ecclesiastes 8 says this:

"Who is like the wise? And who knows the interpretation of a thing? A man's wisdom makes his face shine, and the hardness of his face is changed. I say: Keep the king's command, because of God's oath to him. Be not hasty to go from his presence. Do not take your stand in an evil cause, for he does whatever he pleases. For the word of the king is supreme, and who may say to him, 'What are you doing?' Whoever keeps a command will know no evil thing, and the wise hear will know the proper time and the just way. For there is a time and a way for everything, for though a man's trouble lies heavy on him. For he does not know what is to be, for who can tell him how it will be? No man has power to retain the spirit, or power over the day of death." (vv. 1-8a)

There have been so many days in my life when I have questioned the Lord's purpose. Most of my time in high school and early in college was spent unable to see why he had me in a position of singleness. When I started college, it seemed like I was surrounded by couples. So many of my friends came to college and immediately found someone, and it still seems like so many of my friends are getting married, when in reality a very small number of them are getting married, and even then, the large majority of these friends are a lot older than me.

And then there was me. I had great friends who I can imagine will remain my friends for my entire life, and it always seemed like something would come very close to happening for me, and then I would get my hopes up only to have them dashed to the ground. I would have one good day when I felt extremely confident in who I was, and then the next day it seemed like nothing was going right. It seemed like my world was falling apart. I spent a lot of time asking God why he had me in this place, but I didn't ask with the right mindset.

My vision was cloudy. It's like Satan has stolen my glasses that allow me to see with something like twenty-twenty vision, leaving me to struggle to make out anything. I couldn't look to the past because I couldn't see it, and so I was left with my seemingly subpar present circumstances, and those just didn't seem to be enough. I would tell myself that it would be so much better if I was in a relationship. It would be so much better if I had a better job. It would be so much better if I was smarter. If I was more attractive. More successful. More anything.

What I really seem to be seeking is something *more* than right now. With that mindset, nothing will ever be good enough. No matter what my status is when I get married, no matter how well I age, no matter what kind of job I get when I graduate from college, no matter how successful I am, nothing will ever satisfy. That is a rather sad life to lead. Living in discontentment with the present, hoping that maybe tomorrow will be better, is settling for a life of just that: hoping. And that's not the good kind of hope, either. This is the kind of hope that will likely go unquenched. This hope is nothing more than a wish. This hope in the illusion of the overarching power of time will always, without fail, end in disappointment. Placing our hope in Christ to fulfill His promises to us in His own time is something that will be difficult, but it is worth it because it opens us up to a world where hope goes way beyond a mere wish for something better. Wishes have a negative connotation in my mind, because by calling something a "wish," then you're automatically giving it the opportunity not to come true. Hope is more reliable than that. Hope is a wish with a foundation, and when the foundation of your wish is something that cannot be overpowered, then it's easy to call your wish real hope.

Because I go to a Christian college, I'm required to take a class on the Old Testament and a class on the New Testament in order to graduate. The second semester of my freshman year, I found myself in an Old Testament Introduction class, and with that class came the required Bible-reading. As an English major, I'm up to my ears in reading that's due tomorrow or the next day, so reading that's due in a month, though it may be all of Genesis and Exodus, tends to fall through the cracks. So there I found myself, a week out from the exam with essentially all of Genesis and Exodus still to be read on top of the readings due in my other classes. In my reading, though, I realized that I identify with a character of the Bible that I often disregard because she's so early in the Scriptures and so familiar: Sarah. In all my worrying about *when* God is going to come through for me— though that's a futile question to even ask— I failed to look to the Scriptures concerning the woman who waited decades—literally decades— for a child. She tried everything. When God told her that she was going to have a child, she couldn't help but laugh. God had waited so long, how could he possibly come through now?

> "They said to him, 'Where is Sarah your wife?' And he said, 'She is in the tent.' The Lord said, 'I will surely return to you

about this time next year, and Sarah your wife shall have a son.' And Sarah was listening at the tent door behind him. Now Abraham and Sarah were old, advanced in years. The way of women had ceased to be with Sarah. So Sarah laughed to herself, saying, 'After I am worn out, and my lord is old, shall I have pleasure?' The Lord said to Abraham, 'Why did Sarah laugh and say "Shall I indeed bear a child, now that I am old?" Is anything too hard for the Lord? At the appointed time I will return to you, about this time next year, and Sarah shall have a son.' But Sarah denied it, saying, 'I did not laugh,' for she was afraid. He said, 'No, but you did laugh.'" (18:9-15)

She couldn't help but laugh. She thought the Lord was being silent and ignoring her, but the Lord was working. He was making things happen in his own timing, and that is the best timing. I can't help but put myself in her shoes and know that, for one thing, my situation could be a lot worse, and for another thing, The Lord is at work in time. He is teaching us patience in the waiting times and trust in the trying times. He is teaching us that even the circumstances that seem laughable are possible because He is working all things out for our good and His glory.

Sometimes I think about things that I'm looking forward to in life—like getting married or getting hired at some swanky organization where I can just write and design things all day and get paid for it—and I can't help but think that the likelihood of those things actually happening is something that is, indeed, laughable. That just shows my lack of trust in God and my lack of faith that He will come through for me with His own perfect purposes in His own perfect time. Honestly, that should be an exciting concept for Christians because it means that we have Heavenly paradise to look forward to even when it seems as if we have completely lost our way. We have complete glorification and eternal life with Christ to look forward to in spite of how we doubt God and His ability to give us things we need or want. Not only is that a humbling concept, but that is also an exciting concept that makes me laugh for joy rather than with disbelief.

I spent an entire season of life wishing I wasn't in that season of life. I was depression's doorstep, and I couldn't see why on earth God had me where he had me. Now, though, I look back on that time and I can see what God was doing. He was making me learn to be thankful for my struggles, and that's a lesson I've held close to my heart for a lot of years. When you're able to take a situation in your life and see it from a bird's-eye perspective, it's not that hard to see all the amazing things God has done and is doing. I'll admit that in the moment it is so hard to see what God is doing in the dry times, but when that rain comes, it'll coat your body in it's sweet relief, and you'll be free.

Comfortable

If I enter into a situation in which I don't have full knowledge of what's happening, my palms begin to sweat, everything surrounding me slows down, and I feel like I'm having a mini panic attack. I can't handle it when I don't know. It's as if every time I don't know something, I just assume that the worst is going to happen, that I'm going to fail, that I'm going to suffer, that I'm going to be inconvenienced, that God's plans are to harm me and not to give me a future, or that God's plans for me are for His own good and He just doesn't care about my well-being. I know that was a run-on sentence, but that's a lot like my thoughts in real time. My mind travels at one hundred panicking miles per hour and makes a thousand run-on sentences-sentences-worth of bad scenarios.

During the first semester of my freshman year of college, I went to an event, and it ended up being an event at which I had to speak a little bit about a subject in which I'm not incredibly confident. As soon as the speaker explained the proceedings, I began to panic. I closed my eyes and thought, *I cannot have a panic attack right now.* So I opened my eyes again, I sucked it up, I participated, and I enjoyed it.

I noticed in going home for the holidays that I long for the comfort of my room back at school because all of my stuff is there. I don't have to live out of a suitcase. I can walk for two minutes and grab a meal for free, I can go study in the library for a change of scenery, I can walk out of my hall and into the lobby of my building to hang out with my friends. When I'm home, it's great to be around my family, but my best friends live two or more hours away from me, and I have to spend money to get a change of scenery, or run the risk of rudely sitting in a coffee shop without buying anything. It's safe to say that there is a certain sacrifice that comes with change, and a large part of that sacrifice is a loss of comfort. Even in moving into my dorm, there were certain things I gave up: privacy, silence (which I learned that I don't love as much as I thought), the luxury of having all of my stuff right there with me, among other things. My summer with working at a day camp brought me so much change, and that was definitely uncomfortable for me. I felt very alone in this. I felt like everyone else was having an easy time adjusting to sharing a bed with someone different every week, and I was left in my insecurity about how much I move around in my sleep. That fact threatened to ruin my entire summer. It was uncomfortable to live in a hotel, and after ten weeks of living with three or four people per week, I realized how discomfort led to growth, even though it wasn't exactly enjoyable in the moment.

I also love tradition. I love the idea of being surrounded by family during the holidays, going to church and hearing a talk about the Advent season around Christmastime. I love leaving out a cookie or two for Santa on Christmas Eve, even though I'm an adult. I love waking up on Christmas morning and still not being allowed to open gifts until we read *The Boy Who Laughed at Santa Claus* and let my parents open their gifts.

But recently, a lot of the sentimental traditions within my family have changed. I tried to FaceTime my family to do our first Advent devotion of the season my freshman year of college, and I couldn't get through because neither of our WiFi connections were very strong. I missed my brother's birthday. My Grandmama has long since moved out of her house, and Thanksgiving and Christmas morning are never the same since my childhood memories of playing in her basement with my cousins are very much in the past. In addition, she lived in an assisted living home and then a nursing home for a while, and wasn't able to remember who I was for a lot of the time toward the end of her life. The number of people who attend our family Thanksgiving have significantly decreased since I was younger, and the number of people who attend our Christmas morning celebration, now held at my house, has drastically decreased as well.

This doesn't only hold true for the holiday season. Over the summer, we rarely take family vacations anymore. When we are together, we argue. We don't have family nights any more. I spent eleven weeks away from home, and my family went on without me. I missed family vacation for two summers in a row. I missed the last of our family breakfasts on Saturday mornings with my grandmama. I disrupted tradition with life.

But why do I find so much joy and fulfillment in the material side of the season? Why am I saddened at the end of certain, long-held traditions, even though I know I'll make new traditions eventually?

It seems like my childhood is fading away, and it's taking my joy with it. Reality is setting in all at once, and it's completely unfamiliar. Whenever something goes away or changes, that creates a little spark of fear in my heart that nothing is ever going to be the same again. That fear burns into a little flame, and if I don't stop it, it just spreads throughout my attitude, my face, and my being. I become someone who is living fear of change, and I become someone who is living in fear of commitment because of the fact that nothing lasts forever. Comfort gets too comfortable, and it changes too quickly.

Comfort is a beautiful thing, but it is explicitly listed in the Bible as one of the things we must give up in order to be followers of Christ. That is not to say that it is wrong to be at peace. But if the Lord called me out of my warm, fleece sheets into the cold, rainy outdoors to help someone out, I think I would be less than enthused to go. That's the danger of comfort: it's addictive. It grows on you to the point where anything less than comfort simply doesn't live up to the standard you've set, and then you're miserable.

That's why it's so much harder, in my opinion, to begin maturing in your faith when you're older. As we age, our standard for comfort grows with culture's standards, and as that standard gets higher and higher, we become less and less tolerant of anything less than it. Ease seems to be a given. It doesn't come across as the privilege that it truly is— when I worked at a day camp for a summer, I realized I took even my own bed for granted. When the Lord throws trials our way, we assume that He's out to get us, and we are more likely to lash out at Him and get angry than seeing trials as opportunities to grow. Even as someone who I feel is somewhat mature in my faith, when I feel uncomfortable I'm quicker to question God and be frustrated with Him than to ask why and ask how I can grow. That's just my human nature.

Some days I get this feeling in my gut just like I felt when the Spirit was speaking to me to tell me to do a hard thing, and I get worried. What could the Lord want me to give up now? He already caused me to go through such a tough time getting over a guy, and he caused me to feel so uncomfortable and insecure for so many months afterward. The blame begins to sprout from my lips into my prayers, it makes its way to God, and it stays planted there.

My brother and I used to play in the woods surrounding our house when we were younger, and since we just sort of placed our house in the middle of nowhere, the woods are pretty overgrown. There were a few clear areas, though, and those areas were prime real estate for forts that we grossly overestimated in our minds. As a result of probably many people attempting to clean out the woods and failing, there were and still are piles and piles of limbs and vines just thrown together— something my dad rumored to my younger brother and me to be hiding a treasure. Underneath all those vines and sticks was apparently something priceless. But to get to the center of the pile would be quite a task. We were content stealing limbs from the outer edges to build our forts, but sometimes those limbs would be stuck—attached to the pile by tangled vines and roots that seemed to never want to be moved. As we left the piles to grow over the years, those outer edges slowly but surely ceased to be the outer edges, and those limbs we once tried to remove from the pile have since become overgrown with more tangled branches.

I say all this to say that as I blame God for my problems out of my own immature faith, that blame takes root, and it continues to grow, hiding the treasure that is our Savior. It creates Him into something that we can't seem to reach because we are too busy blaming Him for creating all these bad circumstances. We are too busy calling Him out for stealing the comfort that was never ours in the first place. With maturity in faith comes the ability to see discomfort as a blessing. As we grow into more spiritually sound Christians, we are able to see more like Christ, and that means that we are able to see our difficult times as times when we are able to see hope for even more growth in our faith. It turns those times into opportunities for growth rather than sinking deeper into our situation.

I can confidently say that I have yet to make it to this point in my faith. I still sometimes see hard circumstances as things that were meant to hurt me, but at the same time I am finding myself sometimes looking to the Throne of God to find answers. Those moments when I absent-mindedly turn to God for my answers are my favorite moments because, for a moment, they give me a small burst of pride in my own ability to make it to this point in my spiritual maturity, but then I remember that it absolutely is not me who is changing the trajectory of my life—it's God. God is changing me from the inside out, and it's beautiful what He's been able to do with such a broken human.

I remember when I was in high school, I finally figured out that I had to be thankful for my struggles or I would be absolutely miserable. God doesn't just give us good things that we love. He also gives us things we may not necessarily enjoy, but the reward we receive from those things means that our story isn't over just yet.

Existing

I just want you to stop a moment and think about parenting. Imagine that you adopted a child as a toddler. You missed the very beginning of his life, and you were thrust into a very turbulent and difficult time. He is changing a lot, and he is becoming accustomed to his new surroundings, and that leads to tantrums, fits, screaming, chaos. This toddler grows for a few more years, and he starts school. As he begins to prepare to be gone for half the day, you get nervous: Will he cry when I drop him off? Will I cry when I drop him off? Will I have to pick him up halfway through the day because he can't handle it? There are a lot of nerves going in, and all of those questions are answered on the day that you drive up to the school. The crying ensues, and a while later you finally drive away and make do with what you have left of the day before you have to pick him up.

Your child who you took into your home makes messes. He gets sick and you have to clean up after him. He yells at you. He "borrows" your stuff and never returns it. He costs you countless dollars in tuition, sports fees, doctor bills, dentist bills, grocery bills, car insurance, and so much more, and I'm sure I would be able to think of more if I was actually a parent. He costs you more emotionally, though. You cry because you don't know if he actually loves you. You cry because you don't know if he's going to make the right decisions when you let him go out on his own. You worry when he doesn't make it home before his curfew and hasn't contacted you. You worry when he leaves the house until he comes home that night. You worry when you send him to bed if he'll go to sleep and wake up the next day or if that was the last time you'd see him. You worry about his spiritual life. You cry because you think he's looking at things he shouldn't be looking at in his room when he says he's doing his homework. You cry because, when you find out he is doing that, you don't know what to do about it. You're angry because that girl he started dating is kind of sketchy. You don't know how much control is too much control when he's at that awkward age between childhood and adulthood. You cry because you are angry at him. But you never kick him out. The last time he failed was not the breaking point. You still love him, even when you don't like him, even when you're disappointed in him, even when you're angry at him, even when you don't know if you can trust him, even when you're annoyed by him.

Then he cleans up. He changes his life and gets back on the right track. You stop crying because you wonder if he's doing the right thing, and you start crying because he's going to college soon. He's going to leave the nest. That toddler you adopted and fostered and loved is going to leave your arms and go out into the arms of the world. You wonder if he'll make it. You wonder if he'll be back home because he can't handle it (or because you can't handle it). You wonder if you can trust him. You wonder if you can trust God.

God adopts us into his family whenever we answer his call, and he loves us more than any parent could ever love their child. We make messes. We sin. We disappoint him when he gives us a thousand chances to change, but he never stops welcoming us back into his arms. He never stops being the parent who goes into their son's room at night after he finally made it home and fell asleep just so they can pray for their son and be in the same room as them without any fighting for once. He never stops wanting us, even when we don't want him. He never stops speaking to us, even when we've long since stopped listening. He never stops letting us exist, even when we don't deserve to exist.

It was week four of my summer working with the day camp, and Monday came and went without a hitch. I thought I had the greatest group of campers I'd had all summer. They were the perfect combination of fun and quiet, athletic and artsy, mature and a little less mature. Since I worked with completed fifth and sixth grade kids, it was a hit or miss some weeks as to whether or not they would want to participate in camp culture, and this week I had already decided that my campers loved camp, which made it easier for me to love my job. They listened well during my small group lessons and during the large group sessions. They were awesome, and I told them that.

The next day, though, was a different story. I came into the camp day confident, and I left having scolded kids until I just didn't want to do camp any more. They just didn't seem to be listening. They did exactly (literally, exactly) what I told them not to do. If you want real details, we have these banners that are held up by metal poles and metal bases that are basically curtains to make classrooms smaller and more visually appealing, but they're really fragile so they fall pretty easily if kids are leaning against them and pulling on the actual banner. One of my rules is to not touch the banners, and I walked in on my own small group touching the banner, knocking it down, and sending me over the edge. Then I told another one of my groups to stop touching the banner. I looked and immediately someone was pulling on it. I was livid, honestly. And I wanted to quit. In fact, I spent a lot of time thinking I wanted to quit this job and go home. I would never do it, and I do spend the majority of my time loving what I'm doing, but sometimes I just get fed up. Whether that looks like me having to discipline kids until I'm disciplining them in my sleep (that really happened) or me sitting on the floor next to my kids in the dark auditorium worship session crying silently to myself, I sometimes just wanted to give up.

One of the great thing about God is that he never wants to quit. God wants to love us, even though we never deserve it. There is nothing we could do to earn our existence, yet we exist anyway. Also we exist solely to glorify God and love him, but sometimes we don't even do that. Literally, the only two reasons we have to exist according to the Westminster Shorter Catechism are "to glorify God and enjoy Him forever."[4] Yet we don't even speak to him some days. Sometimes we even doubt that he exists. Sometimes we disrespect him. Sometimes we hate him.

But he never stops loving us.

So even when you feel like you don't deserve to be alive, you still get to be alive, and that is all Jesus. That is all because Jesus is the definition of patience and love. He perfectly embodies everything that is good, and that means that we don't have to embody that. We cannot embody it. All we have to do is exist, glorify God, and love God.

It seems a little silly to say that that's "all" we have to do. It's definitely not easy. If we didn't sin or if we didn't live in a sinful world it wouldn't be as difficult. It would be easier to just ignore our own wants and do exactly what God wanted us to do if there wasn't anything around us that seemed more attractive. The sad fact is, though, that there are so many things around us that seem more attractive. Those banners were more attractive to my kids than obeying and getting rewarded for it, although I don't know how. The world is more attractive to the adopted son than making his parents pleased with him. Existing on our own is sometimes more attractive than existing with God.

Yet he still lets us exist. I wish I, myself, could understand the gravity of that statement. I take my existence for granted.

In Jeremiah 2:13, it says this:
"...for my people have committed two evils: they have forsaken me, the fountain of living waters, and hewed out cisterns for themselves, broken cisterns that can hold no water."
Not only did the people of Israel just decide to appreciate other things more than they appreciated God, but they also decided to seek fullness in other things completely separate from God. They created these containers for water that would not hold any water. It's not just that, though: these cisterns *could not* hold water. They couldn't do it if they tried. They were broken—irreparable by their own two hands.

We exist as broken cisterns. We keep trying to be full, but every time we pour into ourselves with something besides Christ, it slowly leaks out. It seems like we're full for a little bit, but eventually, without us knowing, all that had once made us full has leaked out onto the ground, useless. When we base our existence on glorifying Christ, though, we are full— in fact, we are overflowing. He mends the holes in our cisterns by gently covering them with his grace and mercy. He fills the gaps because he is the bridge. He mends the wounds because he is the Healer. He allows us to exist as repaired cisterns because he loves us deeply and doesn't want the worst for us, just as an adoptive parent does not want the worst for their child, even if their child does everything they can to lose their love.

Some adoptive parents may want to leave their child. Adoptive parents—and parents in general—sometimes do not love their children. It's a real thing. It's part of our existence, tainted by sin, that people do not love other people as much as they should. It's a real problem that there are some adopted children and biological children living in families that either do not love them or just have a hard time showing it. God is bigger than that, though. We exist in a place that is covered in sin, and when we're living apart from Christ, our vision—our entire world— is clouded by sin.

I go to school on Lookout Mountain, and let me just tell you: from January until around the middle of March or April, it's foggy almost every day. And it's not just fog like the kind of fog that you have to turn your bright lights on your car off for; it's like a shroud. During the winter of my freshman year I couldn't even see the building across from mine, and it wasn't that far away. Sometimes I would see someone walking toward me and I wouldn't be able to tell who it was until they got within ten feet of me. I began to feel trapped, claustrophobic, and lost.

That's what it's like when you're living in sin. Your world is cloudy. You can't see any of the goodness in anything because you can't see any purpose behind anything, and because you can't see it, you ignore its presence. You can't see, so you just ignore. Whenever a good thing happens, you write it off, and whenever a bad thing happens, you write it off. It's a tasteless existence.

But, oh, how beautiful life is when the cloud lifts—when April comes and the fog leaves as mysteriously as it arrived. When you can finally see everything around you, and when you can finally see the purpose and beauty in everything that exists, you realize that you exist for a glorious purpose. Accomplishing that purpose makes us full, and when we're not accomplishing that purpose we're just broken cisterns—everything slips through us like sand through an hourglass as our time simply runs out.

One thing I will add, though, is the fact that God did not create us to simply live life. As I've said before, we are called to give God glory, praise, and honor, and part of that is accomplished in enjoying the lives he's given us and enjoying God, himself. We're not just supposed to live life like this is the end, like this is all we have. There is so much more than this.

Fear

Every day is a battle between me and my mind. I'll find myself thinking about something good that happened to me, and then I'll find my mind wandering all the way until it reaches a point where that good thing is no longer good. What if I hurt someone? What if I don't live up to someone's standards? What if I fail?

I do think that a healthy amount of fear is a good thing. I think that being afraid of the right things is important in being good stewards of the lives with which the Lord has blessed us. For example, I lived up in a woodsy area for almost my whole life, and if my brother and I had not been afraid of snakes, then we would be in trouble. However, too much fear is simply too much fear. It inhibits our growth in our faith and it inhibits our sanctification. It steals our necessary trust in our Savior.

For my whole life, and up until she passed away, my Grandmama was intent on all her children and grandchildren standing strongly in trust of Christ. When I was very young, the first money I ever truly earned—one

66

little dollar—was a result of my learning
Proverbs 3:5-6.

"Trust in the Lord with all your heart,
and lean not on your own understanding.
In all your ways acknowledge Him, and
He will keep your paths straight."

Now that I'm in college, I have realized
just how much I desperately need that truth at
the forefront of my mind daily. I realized that I
really don't trust God fully—with my whole heart
— and I find fulfillment in being in control of my
situation. And it is so hard to trust God with
your whole heart. It's not hard to trust him when
things are going well, and it's not hard to trust
him when I feel like I have control. When I lose
that control, though, I find myself stuck in a rip-
current of worry and fear. To trust God with
your whole heart is a significantly harder task.
Anxiety overtakes me like so many waves, and
struggling against it is like struggling against an
actual rip-current: without proper help, the
current only gets worse as our struggle
intensifies. It sweeps our feet out from under us
and drowns us in itself.

At some point, a lifeguard can't save a
drowning swimmer from a rip-current, but the
beautiful thing about God is that He sees all, and
He can rescue all. That's not to say that He will
rescue all, but he has infinite ability to rescue
because he, himself, is infinite.

But sometimes we resist. Sometimes we
fight off the healing hand trying to take control
over our lives as if it doesn't already have
control. Sometimes we try to push away the
grace of God in the midst of the time we need it
most because we think we know better, and that
has consequences. To push away the grace and
healing of God in times of immense fear and
anxiety only serves to cause more anxiety and

plunge us deeper and deeper into the sinking sands: our souls know that we need to worship something, and when we push away the most perfect option we have nowhere else to turn but to an imperfect one.

We are Peter struggling in the waves and the storm. We are Peter plunging deep into fear after he took his eyes off of the one who could make him walk on water. We are Peter, living in fear of what's going on around us rather than taking immense comfort in the one who truly embodies complete comfort. We are Peter before Jesus rescues him from the waves, but we are also Peter after Jesus rescues him from the waves. We are able to renew our trust in Christ because he rescues us every single moment from whatever would threaten us, and imperfectly we run back to him and shift our gaze toward his immense, saving glory.

But what are we worshipping when we actively decide to forsake the most perfect object of worship and trust in something so utterly inferior?

We are worshipping the fear we so hate. We are worshipping the anxiety that gives us a small glimmer of some type of twisted hope that we can begin control of ourselves and our surroundings. We are worshiping what Satan wants us to worship, and in doing so we are giving him what he wants—we're placing ourselves directly in his hands, allowing him to compete with God.

However, we have the opportunity to foil Satan's plan: we simply don't give in to it. We use those opportunities to show him that he doesn't have any control over us, to show him that he isn't in charge of our lives and that he can't win if we trust that God won't let him. Because apart from God, Satan would win every time. Satan would be victorious over our own plan for our lives because our own plans without God's intervention will all inevitably fail. Satan plays off our own failure to convince us that after every failure we make, we are, in fact, failures, ourselves.

Living in anxiety and fear of losing control constantly is simply giving Satan what he wants, but we don't have to do that. We don't have to succumb to the fear placed in our path. We have the beautiful ability to put our trust in something so much bigger, so much more powerful, and so much better than our own control, which only leads to anxiety. It's as if Christians know that apart from Christ we are definitely going to fail, so there's this constant tug at our hearts to stop being fulfilled by making our own decisions, by being happy, by succeeding. We seek fulfillment in other things out of worship of the fear we have of failing, being depressed, being unloved, being lost. We seek fulfillment in things that will not only never fulfill us but also will inevitable hurt us. But we just keep grinding on, relentlessly loving a thing incapable of true, steadfast, and unconditional love.

Remembering

When I came to college, I started as a chemistry major because I thought that I wanted to be a chemistry teacher at a small Christian high school like my own. I spent a lot of the end of the summer before my freshman year deliberating between majors, but eventually, I just settled, as I so often do. I justified it by saying that it would be easier to switch out of a chemistry major than into one later on. I really stayed on my track because of the job security it would provide. I knew I didn't want to move on and get my doctorate because I felt called to teach. Or maybe it was that job security thing again. Somewhere deep down inside of me I think I knew I was called to write or teach (not chemistry), but the term "starving artist" terrified me.

After the first day of my first chemistry course, I was happy with my decision, but as we delved further and further into the material, I became unsure. I realized that I had no idea what I was doing. I was lost in a world of dangerous chemicals and stoichiometry, and I suddenly began to realize that I had not learned any new chemistry since I was a freshman in high school, which meant that I'd been a little ambitious in saying that I loved chemistry. Maybe this was a mistake. People asked me if I was only switching majors because of the difficulty of the major, and people asked me if I felt uncomfortable being a chemistry major, and I didn't really know how to respond to either question. I didn't want to change majors solely because I was too lazy to try hard, and I didn't just want to change majors because I had some weird feeling. I wanted it to be the right decision because, like most people, I crave being right. Soon after, anxiety began to set in. I asked for opinions, and most of the people I asked told me that I should switch to whatever I felt God calling me to do. It seemed like something of a cop-out, but I trusted those people. In reality, I needed to spend more time listening to God, even though it seemed like of odd since I wasn't hearing anything. But God is always speaking.

Flash forward to about a month into the semester, and I was dead-set on changing my major. I had been through a few labs, and I decided chemistry just wasn't for me. I really wasn't comfortable in the lab, so I definitely would not be comfortable teaching kids how to be comfortable in a lab. Now, I'm an English major, which is where I truly think the Lord is calling me. When I registered for my second semester classes, I don't think I had ever been so excited to learn. This was likely the most I had ever felt at peace about a decision since I decided to come to Covenant College, and that's saying a lot, since I rarely feel comfortable making decisions. The Lord brought me a peace that I absolutely did not deserve considering how much I doubted him, but I welcomed it with loving arms. It felt like I had reached the peak of my college career, and it was only the middle of my first semester of freshman year.

One day near the end of my first and only semester of college-level chemistry, I woke up and went to clock in for my eight-AM shift, then I finished my work, clocked out, and went back to my room. With a particularly difficult-seeming lab in my midst, I tried to make the best of my small amount of free time. I went to eat breakfast and have my quiet time as I usually did on my slow Thursday mornings after work, and as I pulled out my journal to write, I began to dwell on the lab. I began to dwell on the fact that, since I spilled at least ten milliliters of lightly concentrated hydrochloric acid on my hands during the last lab, I would likely spill some on my hands in this lab, too, and this stuff was going to be more concentrated— concentrated enough to actually damage me. My mind raced, and my body was trying in vain to catch up.

The room began to slow down around me, and I couldn't focus on what I was doing. I was lost in my thoughts, and I felt as if I could burst into tears at any moment. I felt helpless. My thoughts were eating away at me, and I was letting them as I sat in a silent panic in the back of our dining hall. I couldn't seem to pull myself out of this. I usually am able to pull myself out of anxiety with various self-care methods, but I couldn't jump over the hump of the initial fog that comes with anxiety attacks.

Eventually, after I spent a few hours in a weird stupor, I told my roommate I couldn't do the lab, and I began to sob. Then I called my mom—a conversation in which I didn't do much of anything but sob. I realized that this was a problem, so I skipped the lab, and emailed my professor, hoping that he would understand. Part of me hoped that he would just let me accept failure and bypass the lab. I talked to one of my friends about it, and he told me that he thought my grade could handle it because somehow I wasn't doing badly in the lab, even though I wasn't very good at it. I felt some semblance of relief as I realized that I may be able to just move on with my life and not have to do too many more labs this semester, but I also felt some guilt for quitting right in the middle of the challenge just because I didn't think I could handle it on my own.

I often regret the fact that I started college as a chemistry major just so that I could be guaranteed a job, steady pay, and stability. I craved knowing. I craved comfort. I craved security and happiness in a bright, full future. I didn't look to the Cross for my answers, and I didn't seek out the Lord's will for my life before I went in: I just went for it because, even though I wasn't fully on board with it, I figured it would be safe. If I wasn't a chemistry major, my schedule would have been easier. I wouldn't have had an anxiety attack before a lab that left me exhausted for an entire day and caused me to miss two shifts of work and do poorly on an exam in a different class the next day. I wouldn't have had all the stress of studying for quizzes every week over information that I didn't really understand. I wouldn't have studied for seven hours for a very short exam to receive a low grade in return. I wouldn't have studied almost to the point of tears for my final exam.

There's always another side, though. "However" is a weighty word, and it has defined my life for years.

I wouldn't have met one of my best friends on my major-specific orientation team. I wouldn't have learned how to better deal with my anxiety by confronting it head-on. I wouldn't have learned how to ask for help when I'm at my most vulnerable. I wouldn't have had meaningful conversations with my chemistry professor while I was explaining to him what happened and while I was making up the lab I had to miss. I wouldn't have grown into who I am today.

The Lord calls us to remember, especially in the hard times, the times when He so obviously came through for us in a huge way. We are called to remember that He will also come through for us every time we need Him, and even when we think we don't. He calls us to reflect on the times when He brought us out of sorrow into the revival that is His incomparable joy. He calls us to remember what He has done, and acknowledge the fact that He can and will do it again. We need only to trust in His promises and believe in His infinite ability and longing to get the job done and work all things out for our good.

I'm not here to tell you it's easy, though. I'm not here to tell you that once you become a Christian it's easy to remember what God has done for you. In the moment, it's hard. It's so difficult because on top of the fact that you can't seem to get out of the rut you're in, you wonder why God would put you in that rut in the first place. Working at a Christian day camp, I found myself in a rut. I started out the summer feeling like it was just a job. I would have occasional fun, but doing motions on stage during all the songs was a drag, leading cheers was stressful because I wasn't ever sure which one I was supposed to do, teaching games was hard because I wasn't ever good at the recreation part of our day. The only thing I found joy in at the beginning was teaching kids about Jesus, but even then, I struggled. Some days, I felt like I wasn't cut out for the job. My first Monday ended, and I didn't even know what had happened to me. I couldn't remember the lesson I had taught because I was so nervous, and the fact that our lunches got mixed up and I didn't get one until it was time to leave for the next thing wasn't a big deal because I was so nauseous that I couldn't even eat the granola bar I'd gotten that morning. So for the first couple of weeks of the summer, my job was just that: a job. I was working toward week ten, and any "success" I had along the way was just another stepping stone on my path to the end of the summer. But then, we encountered our first very large camp, and my perspective changed. It was one of the best weeks of the entire summer. I realized that I was actually having fun, and that was the week that I performed the best as well. I realized that God was working, even though none of my kids had ever accepted Christ to that point. I realized that God was working, even though I never felt poured into until the very end of that week. However, then I went through week four and five, and I realized that what I thought could not be any more fun could actually be. I realized that I could have fun, minister to kids, and get paid all at the same time. During those weeks, I got a very large glimpse of why I was employed there, and that caused me to love my job.

But then, I got too many glimpses of home, and I became homesick. I remembered the summer before when I spent a month living in want of my own bed, my own room, and freedom to go wherever I wanted. In this case, I was remembering all the times I had enjoyed myself and longing to be back there. I got to see my boyfriend, and I longed to be back at school where I could see him every day. I longed to be at a camp where kids were truly passionate about camp and the Gospel. I longed to be around my school friends who knew my life. I longed to be where I wasn't, and so, mentally, I wasn't there.

I had a rough seventh week, even though the church where we were serving was awesome, and I let that get to me. After the steak lunch our hosts served us, I felt momentarily happy, but then I realized how many more weeks we truly had left, and I returned to my original state of being miserable. Hanging out with my campers was a drag, and leading cheers brought me no joy. I spent an entire week letting little things get to me, and I rekindled the negative fire that had burned inside me for so long. That opened the door to exhaustion and anger. I resented the fact that I ever decided to take the job.

The eighth week began with church, and I couldn't even pay attention to what was happening because I was so distracted by the fact that I thought my relationship with God was falling apart, I thought my relationship with my boyfriend was falling apart, I thought I'd never make it back to a point where I could have fun doing my job because I was exhausted and everything hurt— literally, it was a struggle to get out of bed in the morning. I was dwelling on the moment I was living in, and I forgot all the kids I'd had in the past seven weeks who had made an impact on my life. I forgot all the things I'd seen God do that made me question why I doubted him in the first place— like the simple fact that some kids love camp so much that they can't stand it. I forgot all the fun I'd had back at the beginning— like when I had painted my entire face green on one occasion and blue on another and then had to dance on stage in front of a room full of kids (and some adults). It became a job again, and it became a job I wanted to quit right then and there. I let the frustration get to me, and I let all those facts I just listed discourage me from the fact that God had me there for a reason and that the summer was truly something I would never forget because it was so much fun. I let them discourage me from remembering all the discomfort I had felt in the past that God had used to speak to me in beautiful ways and minister to my heart.

I just forgot, and I began to live in the moment too much. So I say all this to say that it isn't easy to remember. In fact, it's almost painful to remember because in order to see God's work, you have to start with the "before" picture, and sometimes we just get stuck there. It's easy to live in discomfort and just allow that marinate and grow and get stronger and stronger.

Seeking fullness in what is happening right now, at this very moment, in our lives will only bring heartache after a while. Our current circumstances do not have the power to fulfill us nearly as well as God can because they are fleeting and fickle. Once we come to terms with that, we can stop dwelling on those circumstances. Yes, it seems like the end of the world sometimes—like we just couldn't go on if we tried—but that is where the beauty of the hand of God comes into play. He is always working, but he has a way of interjecting so loudly, flipping everything we've ever known upside-down exactly when He knows we need it, not necessarily when we think we need it. He does what He does for a reason, and we can take comfort in that when we look back and see the reason for past difficult circumstances.

We are called to ministry as Christians, and vulnerability is key in showing others the beauty of the grace of God. We have rough past circumstances for many reasons, and one of those reasons is for effective ministry. It doesn't matter how difficult those past circumstances were—from spilling your coffee the moment you walk out of the coffee shop to losing a relative. Everything happens for a reason, which sounds cliché, but it's so true. The truth of this statement transcends the fact that it is overused. People use that phrase as a cop-out, as an alternative to comforting someone, but it only has meaning if you understand that things happen for a reason and then you prayerfully seek out that reason and do what the Lord is calling you to do with your story. Everyone has a testimony whether they see it or not. Even a story that doesn't seem exciting is a story, and your story could be used to speak to other people who don't feel like they have a story either. Personally, I've never felt like I had a story that people wanted to listen to. Nothing too terrible has ever happened to me, and I grew up in a Christian home, so I never went a day without being encouraged in my growing faith. But when I hear stories like mine from people who are like me, but are able to see God's hand in all of that, as well as some kind of significance, I'm always left with some kind of reassurance that no matter how basic my story seems; it can be used and it should be used.

I still struggle, though— as does everyone. Being able to remember what God has done in the past in everyday circumstances reminds me that God will continue to do work through the mundane. In the midst of something hard that's seeming to push me far away from my Savior, it's hard to see the good. It's hard to see God at work when it seems like he's just not working. But God is always at work. When you have a bird's-eye view of a situation after it's already all played out, it's easier to see what God has done, and God gives us the ability to see things that way in order to point us back to His sovereignty over our entire lives. He wants us to know that he's always working, and he uses the past to show us just that.

Remembering your past is key to ministry, and it's key to seeking fullness in Christ. When you solely look at your present, you can easily become dissatisfied with the Lord because it doesn't seem like he's working. In reality, God is always working, and when you can get a bird's-eye view of the trajectory of your life, then it gives you a mind-blowing affirmation of the faith you thought was wavering. Remembering your past, remembering decisions you made, remembering your successes and failures, remembering your best moments and your worst moments all work together to give us yet another great reason to trust in Christ for fullness and satisfaction.

What Makes Me Full

What makes me full is, simply put, the work of Christ on the cross.

I will say this: I'm not perfect, and neither are you. Without immense faith in Christ, we could not feel content in the work He has done because on the outside it doesn't seem like much is happening. On the outside it just seems like Christians get the short end of the stick all the time, and that makes people not want to follow God. That makes us look undesirable. But when you pay attention to the implications of Christ's work on the cross, it becomes something of which everyone should want to be a part, even though not everyone does.

On my own, apart from Christ, I could see all the beauty, sacrifice, and selflessness in the world and still not believe in who God is, and that was a sad existence now that I look back. When you don't know why things are beautiful, you don't know what you're missing until you fill in that piece. But with His influence on my life, I'm able to use those instances of common grace to amplify my vision of the miracle of the cross, and the mess that is my life starts to look a little less empty and a little more beautiful.

How do you get fulfilled? That was the question crossing my mind for much of my time in middle school. I honestly have no idea why that was the question I had (other than God preparing my mind for what he was always planning to teach me), but I never really found an answer for it, so I stopped mulling it over and pushed it to the back of my mind.

Think about this: what if everything you've ever worked for, every gain you've ever made, everything you've ever owned was meaningless? It sounds like a pretty depressing life to lead. Nothing you do matters. Nothing you gain matters. Nothing you own matters. Nothing matters.

Except God.

When I worked hard at something and someone doesn't care about it or someone tells me it's worthless, I get angry. I see the value in what I do, and when someone contradicts that value, I get defensive. Why did I work for something if I had no hope of it ever being truly appreciated? Why did I take risks if there was no way that I was going to actually get the reward I'd hoped for? It seems pointless to me to work for something and never get it, and that's how it would be if we didn't have Christ. If God didn't exist, then nothing we ever did would matter in the grand scheme of things. In Ecclesiastes it talks about the fact that all we humans have in life apart from Christ is to enjoy our time and work here on earth. But when people are eternally without Christ, then, yes, they can enjoy their work on earth because of common grace, but there's always going to be something missing. The reason Christians are still called to enjoy the earth (just not to seek satisfaction in it) is because it is a gift from God. We don't have to live without a purpose. If we didn't trust in Christ with all we had, then that would be a very sad, purposeless existence. So all the things we have and all the people we love mean nothing apart from Christ, and that's the reality of the situation.

Though it seems slightly depressing to not care about anything you have because of the inherent meaninglessness of it all, it should also be relieving. It should come as an encouragement to us that we are not tasked with making our own joy out of mere things.

We would inevitably fail every time.

"Vanity of vanities, says the Preacher, vanity of vanities! All is vanity."

These words in the first verse of Ecclesiastes, chapter one, say one thing, and it's what I said earlier: nothing means anything. All is meaningless, like wind, fleeting away in less than a moment. Before you can grab onto it, it's gone, never to be seen again. In the second chapter of Ecclesiastes, the first ten verses the Preacher's description of all that he had. He had "great works," "houses," "fruit trees," "male and female slaves," "singers," and even "wisdom" straight from God, yet he was still at a loss. What did it all mean?

Nothing.

Verse eleven says this:
"Then I considered all that my hands had done and the toil I had expended in doing it, and behold, all was vanity and a striving after wind, and there was nothing to be gained under the sun."

"There is something hollow and unsatisfying about all this,"[5] according to a commentary by James Limburg. The Preacher knew that nothing he had could ever measure up to what God provides for us. Yes, he addresses the fact that worldly things can and should make us happy. In Ecclesiastes, chapter eleven, verses seven and eight, he says,

> "Light is sweet, and it is pleasant for the eyes to see the sun. So if a person lives many years, let him rejoice in them all; but let him remember that the days of darkness will be many. All that comes is vanity."

A commentary by William P. Brown argues this:

> "Knowing the prime of one's life, along with its accompanying blessings of heart and prosperity, is fleeting only underscores the import of joy... Such is the key to human existence for the sage: to relinquish control over life in order to be freed for joy"[6].

Yes, love worldly things, but don't value them more than Christ. Don't let them take God's place, and don't allow them to decrease your love for the Savior.[7] That's where my testimony starts to pick up.

I was dealing with immense loneliness. I was stuck in what seemed like an inescapable pit, dark and deep, from which nothing and no one could pull me. I felt depressed, I felt abandoned, I felt lost. Nothing I did ever seemed to work out, and because of that I was drawn away from the One who completes every task and brings it to fulfillment. The night that I stumbled on Psalm twenty-two, it spoke to me in ways that no Scripture had ever spoken to me before. Before, I felt like there were knives stabbing straight into my heart, mutilating everything I had ever believed about myself and God.

Verse twenty-four says this:
"For he has not despised or abhorred the affliction of the afflicted, and he has not hidden his face from him, but has heard, when he cried to him."

The knives slip out of their place deeply lodged in my heart, and the wounds close with the gauze of grace and Godly provision. When I felt loved by no one, the Lord met me in the form of His Word. He found me in the thorns that pricked my heart and let my joy spill out. He found me in the rubbish that I thought constituted my entire being. He was and is continuing to be the holy solution to my regrets, anxieties, fears, and doubts by mending my holes and refilling what was once empty. He wasn't ever planning on leaving me in my fear and pain. He wasn't ever planning on leaving me in tears. Even when it doesn't feel like God is working to pull you up out of the muck, He is. He is the perfect solution to every single mess that we are, and He loves to help us out. He loves to pull us out of what's holding us back and place us at his righteous right hand. It's a glorious moment when we find ourselves in a place of value and security when we were once in a place of nothingness and purposelessness. That's how God works.

I'm not perfect and you're not perfect. When I say all these things, know that I don't listen to my own words as if they are even close to being perfect, and you can't either. Whatever the Spirit led me to write, know that my communication is imperfect, and your absorption of the information is also imperfect. But His inspiration is perfect. Let that make you appreciate the perfection of Christ and His love and grace even more than you already do.

When you seek fullness in something other than Christ, then you have nothing to gain. I sought fullness in being attractive, and I was let down by my imperfect appearance. I sought fullness in being smart, and I was let down by people simply doing better than me on assignments. I sought fullness in another imperfect human being, and I was let down by his imperfection as well as my own faults. I sought fullness in having a "put together" life and I am continuing to be let down by the fact that time is slipping away, and I'm still worshipping it. Apart from Christ, I am one imperfect mess, failing moment after moment, slipping further and further away from rescue.

But God.

God contrasts that with His perfection, His love, His completion of our incomplete parts. God contrasts that with every fiber of His being.

Seeing how the Lord is continuing to restore every part of me that is broken gives me hope in the future I have with Him in Paradise. I can look back on all the times I fell short, as humans do. All the times I broke God's laws. All the times I sought satisfaction in something instant yet momentary. All the times I failed and was unable to save myself. I can look back on all those times and praise the Lord for who He is because He is so opposite of me: the most welcome foil to the world's character. I don't even deserve to be alive, yet God sustains me. I don't deserve to succeed, yet He provides. Seeing who Christ has been to me in the past allows me to seek fullness and satisfaction in Him now.

It has had an influence on my perception of His grace as well. Second Corinthians chapter one, verses nine and ten say this:

"Indeed, we felt that we had received the sentence of death. But that was to make us rely not on ourselves but on God who raises the dead. He delivered us from such a deadly peril, and he will deliver us. On Him we have set our hope that he will deliver us again."

In His past grace, we can have a hope in a future grace that will satisfy all needs, heal all hurts, and cure all wants. We can hope in deliverance. In that hope, we should also take on a posture of humility. We are imperfectly searching for this contentment. We are on an imperfect path to being more like Christ. Our imperfect search for identity in Christ should end at the foot of His throne after our all-out sprint to find His grace to make us finally satisfied. We can kneel, heavy-hearted and out of breath, unable to stand on our own any more, and He will meet us there.

Christ came to an imperfect place to meet and save an imperfect people, and He comes and meets imperfect people daily still. He will pick you up, "uphold you with his righteous right hand"[8], and bring you into that place of being so significant you can't even imagine it. In the face of your sin, worry, anxiety, and burdens, He meets you, and he holds you closer than anything, loving you through it all and making you truly and wholly *full*.

Notes

page 5, 1: Lewis, C. S., *Mere Christianity*, (San Francisco: Harper San Francisco, 1952), 141.

page 5, 2: C.S. Lewis, *A Grief Observed*, (Seabury Press: 1980), 90.

page 33, 3: Wayne Grudem, Systematic Theology, (Grand Rapids, Michigan: Zondervan, 1994), 642.

page 60, 4: "Shorter Catechism." The Orthodox Presbyterian Church. http://www.opc.org/sc.html. 25 October 2018.

page 81, 5: James Limburg, *Encountering Ecclesiastes: A Book for Our Time,* Grand Rapids/Cambridge: William B. Eerdman's Publishing Company, 2006. 31.

page 82, 6: William P. Brown, *Ecclesiastes: Interpretation: A Bible Commentary for Teaching and Preaching,* Louisville: John Knox Press, 2000. 104.

page 82, 7: Brown, 104.

page 85, 8: Isaiah 41:10.

Front Cover and Back Cover Image Credit: Natalie Abernathy

41606997R00057

Made in the USA
Columbia, SC
14 December 2018